Words to be spoken

~ A collection of monologues, sketches & plays for performance ~

By

J. L. Dean

Quickbeam Press

Published by Quickbeam Press in 2018

This edition: 2018

This book is a work of fiction. While the places referred to are real the names, characters, and incidents are entirely fictitious. Any resemblance to actual persons, living or dead, is entirely coincidental.

A catalogue record for this book is available from the British Library.

Cover Design by Indie Designz

Print Edition
ISBN-13: 978-0-9927709-8-3

Contents

Women

A Woman's Work

A parody of Lady Macbeth. Eleanor has just received a letter from her husband, as if she hasn't got enough to do....

Eleanor:

Husbands are a nuisance, aren't they? Take mine for instance. I won't tell you his name; people tend to get a bit edgy when I mention him, especially in places like this. Let me just say he's in the Scots Brigade, a soldier loyal and true; not at all like the soldiers you hear about in those mucky folksongs. Just listen to me! I call him loyal as though it's a good thing! I suppose it is for those at the top; it's just the quality you want in your subordinates. But when you're trying to persuade your husband to make a name for himself, loyalty can prove a sticking point. I woke him up one night, "Look, darling," I said to him, "I'm only saying this because I love you but it's time you stopped being such a doormat. In this world you have to look after number one". I thought I was quite persuasive but he just rolled over and went to sleep, muttering something about earning his place.

Six months later and he's away fighting in some pointless campaign for a doddery old king. Then I get this letter from him; he's all excited because some old bag lady has told him he's two promotions away from being king. *I've* been telling him that for years but would he listen to me? Oh no, he's got to hear it from some unwashed vagrant before he takes any notice. Still the sceptred orb has, finally, dropped. You'd think I could just order my ermine and sit back wouldn't you? Not with a husband like mine. Just as I think everything's in place he suddenly comes over all squeamish. So, it falls to me to summon the demons, drug the servants, pay the milkman ... I mean, planning's one thing but I hate getting my hands dirty... The more I think about it, the more I think I should dispose of him, as soon as he's disposed of the king – I thought I was going to get that job as well at one point but the old man looks too much like my father. I put my foot down. "To kill the king," I said, "Is one thing. But I won't put a knife into daddy, not even for you." He sulked a bit at that, tried to pretend his eyesight was playing up but I would not be moved. All this effort, just to get my husband onto a throne that should be mine! You see it's alright for a man to have ambition. That's just as it should be. But a woman with drive is called aggressive, unnatural, *fiendish*. It just isn't fair.

Three Little Words

Some girls just never know when they're well off.

Carmel: We've split up, Mike and I. It was very sudden. To be honest I don't really understand what happened. He came home early last week: I remember because I had just broken a nail and I was upset. He was very sweet: he came over and gave me a big kiss; just as I've shown him - above the hairline so he doesn't spoil my make-up. Then he said I deserved some pampering and that he'd booked an hotel. I was so excited I almost hugged him. But he was a bit sweaty from the train. I grabbed the phone to call Jess, so we could plan what we'd take but he said that it was supposed to be a romantic weekend for the two of us so Jess couldn't come. Well, I thought that was really out of order, I mean Jess is my best mate. We go everywhere together. I gave him one of my looks, you know? I had my blue contacts in and my eyes were still red from crying over my nail so I looked all sweet and vulnerable. It didn't work, he started chatting away about making an early start on Friday – he'd got a day off work as a surprise – and then all the wonderful things we would do. Just him and me. To be honest I can't remember much of what he said, he lost me after the bit about getting up early. Still, I thought; it's a weekend without having to watch him load the dishwasher so why not? Trouble is, I hadn't reckoned on there being quite so much of "him and me". He wouldn't leave me alone for a minute. I managed to find a beauty salon and shake him off for a couple of hours but then he insisted on having dinner together. I wanted to order room service and watch *Casualty* but he wouldn't have it. He'd bought me a dress from the boutique downstairs so I couldn't even wear my own clothes. Well I thought that was bad but all through the meal he kept looking at me and smiling. Then, just as the dessert arrived, he grabbed my hand and held it. He didn't say anything; he just stared at me for ages. Now that's cruel that is. I mean, I've sat through dinner with him and then he grabs my spoon hand just as the profiteroles arrive. I could smell the chocolate under my nose and my mouth was watering so much I thought if he doesn't let go of my hand soon I'm going to start dribbling. Suddenly he did let go, I made a grab for the spoon and had just crammed a profiterole into my mouth when he brought out this little box. He said, "I love you Carmel" and opened it. There was a diamond ring inside and I thought, "Oh my God. That's far too small". I just sat there, sucking the chocolate sauce off my teeth listening to him propose. Then he asked me to say something. Well, what he actually said was "I want to hear you say the three most important words in life", his voice was all soft and wobbly. I was a bit confused, he'd been making me drink champagne all night but it was an easy enough question. Well, it was obvious wasn't it? The three most important words in life? Every girl knows that, so I said "Mid-Season Sale". He didn't say anything then, just made a funny choking sound and called for the bill. I had to make my own way home.

Life after Death

After the death of her husband, Catherine confides in a friend.

Catherine:

You know, I almost didn't come tonight. I was afraid I would enjoy myself. Isn't that silly? I was afraid that I would go out and have a good time and forget all about Michael and that if I stopped missing him, even for one evening, that feeling would never return. It's a terrible feeling, I wouldn't wish it on anyone, but holding onto it...it's like proving to myself that I really loved him. If that feeling went away what would be left? I am a widow. I came down to breakfast six months ago and found him dead. He was lying over there, just where the lino's lifting. It was too days before I could cry for him now I feel guilty every time I laugh. Except tonight; I didn't feel guilty tonight. I feel terribly disloyal saying this but in some ways Michael could be pretty boring. He always worked hard but that's all he did and because he'd worked so hard for his money he was very careful about what he did with it: always putting it away for a rainy day. In a way it was a good thing; we always had that security, but it came at the cost of spontaneity. A trip to the theatre was rare indeed and, when we did go, the whole evening was planned with military precision. I shouldn't complain, his life insurance was up-to-date and the mortgage has only another year to go but it's so sad when I think of him saving everything for later and then dying sooner. We were married for ten years but I feel that we never quite *lived* together: never had children, never even redecorated. We had things that others could only dream of; to be honest we had too much, and yet we were never satisfied. We were like souls in Purgatory; constantly striving for some higher existence that we had to earn but could never deserve. What? No, it was never Hell; Michael always believed that we would achieve our aim, whatever that was. I suppose we did achieve something, it's just that we were so obsessed appearing successful that we didn't have much fun on the way. Strange how your perspective changes over time. Let's go into the living room. I still don't feel comfortable in here. My blood runs cold every time I look at that lino.

From: Limbo by Julia Lee Dean. Play text available from Lazy Bee Scripts http://www.lazybeescripts.co.uk/

New Shoes

Melanie talks about her husband's depression and suicide.

Melanie:

I shall never forget the shoes he was wearing. Until the day I die I shall remember them. I'd bought them in the January sales, he'd been very down since losing his job; I thought they'd cheer him up. But he was angry with me for spending the money. He said I had no business spending money on fripperies for him. He actually shouted at me, he'd never done that before. To be honest, it was a relief after all those months of seeing him slumped in front of the TV. That didn't stop me shouting back though. He might have been made redundant but I was still earning and could spend my money how I bloody well liked. I shouldn't have said that. I wish I hadn't said that. Perhaps if I hadn't said that, things might have been different.

He didn't say anything; he just turned up the TV and away from me. He sat in front of the box all evening and never said a word. Something happened to him that night. He was late coming to bed. I was asleep but he woke me up to apologise: not just for that evening but for everything. I said that there was no need but he was insistent. It really mattered to him. He was crying. I told him I loved him and we both cried. That night we made love for the first time in months. I don't just mean sex. We made love: savoured every touch, every taste, as though committing it to memory.

He was still in bed when I left for work the next morning. He watched me as I got dressed. I could see him in the mirror as I put on my make-up. There was something strange about the way he didn't take his eyes off me, as though he were gazing at me from a long way away.

The lights were on when I pulled into the drive that evening but when I called out "I'm home!" no one answered. The television was blaring in the front room as usual but the room was empty. I switched it off and went upstairs, I must have known what he'd done; my legs were like lead as I climbed up, through the silence, to our bedroom. The first and last things I saw were the shoes. Shoe shops never lace shoes properly. I always have to re-lace them but he hadn't done that. The left one looked too loose. I stood and watched it for hours but it never fell. Until the day I die I shall remember those shoes. The way they swung gently in the quiet of the evening. Back and forth. Back and forth. Back and forth.

In My Hands

Lover or stalker?

Eve:

Cross my palm with silver and I'll tell you your fortune. Cross my palm with gold and I'll show you. Oh yes, I'll show you. The human hand is a powerful thing; it can give both pleasure and pain. (*Raises hand, palm outwards*). The hand represents the body in all its parts. (*Points to parts of the hand – see diagram)* Face. Lungs. Spleen. Liver. The sexual organs. Just think of the many intimacies we blithely share with friends, with strangers and the unexplained connections that spring up between unknowing lovers.

It was our hands that brought us together. It was at some party or other, the details are unimportant. What is important is that his hand brushed against mine in the dark and, even without seeing him, all I felt was recognition. There was such certainty, such sympathy between us that there was no need to express it in words. I knew that nothing would keep us apart. It started slowly: we had been one since before we were born. There was no need to rush. I got to know his girlfriend, Jenny. She was a lovely girl, but a distraction. She knew she couldn't hold him and so she let him go. After a fashion. Tragic really. I saw him at the funeral. He was a mess of grief. I smiled at the way he barely looked at me during the service. When he got up to say a few words about Jenny he made such a show of breaking down that I almost doubted him, but at the church door he took my hand, our silent consummation.

We began to meet more often after that. We took great care to meet by chance in unexpected places: at the garage, in town, at the supermarket. He kept up the usual pretence of being surprised to see me and looking quickly around to check that no one was nearby. Of course, he was worried what people would think so soon after Jenny, I didn't push him. One evening I met him at the cemetery. I'd seen him from across the road, going through the gate, his arms full of flowers. He was standing over Jenny's grave. I stood beside him and slipped my hand into his. Such was the spark between us that he sprang away, as though shocked, at my touch. I saw the tears running down his face and reached up to smooth them away. "Soon, we can be together". I whispered, reaching my lips to his. He pulled away from me. His hands were shaking; I took hold of them. I told him that I knew that he didn't want to rush things and that was fine; no one would ever come between us again. He went very still then, I remember the look in his eyes as he turned to the grave and then back to me. Suddenly he wrenched his hands free and pushed me, hard, forcing me to the ground. He was screaming at me. Screaming over and over again, that he hated me, that I had destroyed him; that he never, ever wanted to see me again. I let him walk away from me that night. I watched him hurrying between the graves into the dusk and I let him go. He needs more time.

Mummy's Little Soldier

Rita remembers her son, a soldier killed in Afghanistan.

Rita:

He'd always wanted to be a soldier, even as a little lad. In the evenings, when me and his dad were watching television, he used to come downstairs in his pyjamas, his little face beaming at me as he marched around the front room. Each time he'd halt in front of the telly, stood to attention. We'd carry out a careful inspection of his uniform and then his dad would say, "Now, up the wooden hill to Bedfordshire, quick march!" And he'd run upstairs to bed. I always went up to tuck him in, safe and tight under the blankets. Then I'd say, "Sleep tight, my brave boy. Mummy's little soldier." He loved that, he always smiled as he closed his eyes. And there it was. He'd be a soldier. Even when the other boys stopped wanting to be firemen and train drivers and became teachers and engineers, my boy never wavered.

It's unbelievable now, but it never occurred to me to worry. We knew the risks involved but he'd say, "It's all part of the job, mum." He loved it so much, I had to let go. Afghanistan seemed so far away they might as well have sent him to the moon. He was so excited, bless him. He was doing what he was trained for, he said, making a difference. “You wait, mum”, he said, “I’ll come back a hero - with a medal for gallantry, you see if I don’t!” I was watching the news when I head. Two soldiers had been killed in the south of Helmand province, the newsreader said. Their families were being informed. I remember thinking, “Their poor parents. All those mothers having their world torn apart; beyond all hope of repair. Thank God that isn’t me”. Then the doorbell went.

It was raining as I waited for him at Brize Norton but I couldn’t feel it. I watched the rain running over hands that had aged a hundred years in a week with nothing more than a kind of dull observance. I didn’t want to be there; I didn’t want it to be me there, but I couldn’t bear not to be. I heard the helicopter before I saw it. It lurched out of the sky like some terrible omen but what more could it threaten me with now? I was already dead. When they brought him out there was no parade, no medals. Nothing but the solemn stamp of boots on tarmac; his only decoration was the Union flag he’d fought for. There he was: I couldn’t reconcile my memory of him with the cold anonymous box wrapped in a flag. I knew he was there but it was like looking into an empty space: a hole cut out of the world to show where he should have been. But it wasn’t just an empty space tucked up asleep in that flag. I knocked gently and laid my face against the flag’s fabric, wondering if he had thought of me before he’d closed his eyes that last time. “Sleep tight, my brave boy. Mummy’s little soldier”.

Bad Mother?

The mother of a drug addict defends herself.

Performance note: Maggie is speaking to someone – perhaps a friend or an interviewer – the "beats" and "pauses" are used both to indicate thinking time for Margaret and give the unseen interlocutor time to ask the questions to which Margaret is reacting. There is an opportunity for the actress to demonstrate a variety of emotions in this short passage.

Maggie:

I suppose you think I'm a bad mother. (*Beat)*My son the drug addict. I know what they're saying behind my back; "Problems like that don't come from nowhere and what's she doing about it? Nothing." But they're wrong. It did come from nowhere; I don't know why my son takes drugs. Looking back I can see nothing in his childhood to warn me that one day he'd inject heroin. (*Pause*) Yes, I give him money (*beat*) for drugs; we both know what it's for, why pretend? No, I'm not condoning what he's doing, of course I'm not but I can't beat the addiction... Do you really think I haven't tried? That I wouldn't suck that poison out of his veins with my own mouth if I could? (*Beat*) Then you don't have children. I'm not happy about this; I know that my money could buy the fix that kills him; do you think that hadn't occurred to me?

But you can’t lock a grown man – an addict – in his bedroom and I won’t have him stealing. (*Beat*) If he ends up in prison... (*beat*) game over.

My Best Side

A happy bride becomes an unhappy wife.

Performance Note: the two paragraphs of this monologue take place sometime apart – whether weeks, months or years is up to the performer.

Ruth:

(1) This is my best side. I've decided. I was practicing in front of the mirror for hours last night but this is it. It's definitely my best side, don't you think? So tomorrow, when I go down the aisle, you'll have to stand on the right side. Is that the bride or the groom's side? I don't know! That's bad, isn't it? Oh! I'm getting married tomorrow! I'm getting married to the most gorgeous man! I can't wait for you to meet him, he's lovely; he tells me every day how much he loves me. I'm so lucky to have found someone like him.

(2) No just this side, please. It's better like this. It's not his fault, you know. He does love me. He tells me every day how much he loves me. And how sorry he is. It'll never happen again; he's promised and I believe him. What? Yes, I've thought about leaving, of course I have but where would I go? You see, it's like he says, I'm not strong enough to be on my own. I'm so lucky to have found someone like him.

The Nurse's Lament

Fifteen years after the death of Juliet and her Romeo the Nurse, banished to a Nunnery, remembers

A convent cell. The Nurse sits, asleep, in a chair by a window.

Nuns (*off*): Hail Mary, full of grace, the Lord is with thee:

Nurse : My mistress is the sweetest lady.

Nuns: ... blessed art thou among women and blessed is the fruit of thy womb, Jesus.

Nurse: I think it best you marry with the County...

Nuns: Holy Mary, Mother of God, pray for us sinners...

Nurse: I must needs wake you. Lady, lady, lady!

Nuns: ...now and at the hour of our death. Amen.

Nurse (*waking)*: Amen! Oh, it is the Angelus bell.

I dreamed it was another bell I heard.
Today is Friday, day of sorrows,
now you come to me. Look at them, innocent souls,
hurrying to their devotions.
How easily they move through the dusk:
unburdened by sin, they are guided
by a different light and have no fear of the night.
I wish I had more candles: the darkness
taunts my mind with mortal thoughts of those I loved.
Each of them has gone ahead of me;
you are my only visitors now.
Each of you torment me in different ways.

At least you are here,
my daughter through the loss of my own.
More mine than your mother's.
But will you not look at me, even now?
I can see that I am not forgiven
though you come to me so often.
I cannot bear to hear you weep, ladybird.
I can hear him too, somewhere in the shadows.
You are never without him and I know
that I was wrong, though I hoped to protect you.

You don't understand. How can you?
You were so young and I seemed so old.
How could I know anything of what you felt?
Yet I understand the strength of passion.
I'm an old woman now but still a woman.
Once I was a wife and I enjoyed my husband.
My body hungers for him still. Sometimes,
in my sleep I feel his weight on me.

He calls my name and I wrap my legs around him,
until not even a thought comes between us.
The chapel bell wakes me, empty and unsatisfied.

Everyone I have loved, I have lost.
I can live with the loss, for what is woman's life
but a constant cycle of hope and loss?
But solitude I cannot bear.
I labour with the pain of it day after day
in all its faithful attendance until
every smile is a torment of deception,
every word a triumph of performance.
It is a terrible thing for a woman
to be alone: without life or love
she is nothing but an empty vessel:
a void that is quickly filled with the darker humours.

Those boys, your kin. I remember them.
Bright as blades and just as sharp.
Troubled and troubling. All gone now.
A moment of pointless anger
and a family's future lies dust pale,
staining the street with a lifetime's blood.
And what was the quarrel that caused it?
No one knows: the blow long forgotten
though the injury continued to throb.
I hear from the travellers who rest here,
how things fare in Verona and I fear
the peace won't hold. It has been fifteen years;
those that were children are now young men.
They have listened to the stories of their fathers,
to the songs they sing in drink. The songs
telling tales of courage and defiance.

They listen but they do not hear the price of peace.
They see only the glow of glory
and long to take their party and claim their share.

Tell me friar, for I see you are here too
You who banished me from her chamber.
What was it all for? What has it achieved?
Could you not have shared your aim with me?
Had I known, it could have been different.
And I would have lived these last years loved,
Not alone and prayed over as I am.
I had a name once; then service called me
Now there is nothing but shadows and silence.
I remember it on my husband's lips
when I was a skilled and loving wife.
Will he come to me if I whisper it?

Nurse looks into the darkness and then lifts her head, seeming to smile at someone or something. Clutches her chest, still smiling

Nurse: Angelica

Flesh and Thorns

Louise-Élisabeth Vigée-le-Brun, Marie Antoinette's favourite portraitist, speaks of their last portrait.

***Louise-Élisabeth Vigée-le-Brun*:**

Roses were her flower. She was right to insist on them for the portrait. They matched her in complexion, in grace and in the appearance of simplicity. It is how I like to remember her. Already her popularity was fading. The Queen of France forever a foreign princess. She understood and, child that she was, responded by playing straight into their hands. She looks out from the canvas, her expression sardonic, holding her flower, a ribbon between flesh and thorn. Yet it is what I see in her eyes that stills. Did she *know*? Was it really such a short step from the *libelles* to the mob and, finally, their sharp-tongued Madame? How imperceptibly it began, yet ten years; ten little years was all it took for a mistreated people to rise in support of new manipulators.

Should I have taken more care? The dress I had her wear; it was not her shift, as the scandal-mongers screamed, but something in the new style of dress that followed her own shape instead of pressing her into another's ideal. Yet a dress is as significant as the woman who wears it. We were foolish to look for freedom there.

It was not my last portrait of her; a queen is forever portrayed, theirs is a cruel and curious immortality. Yet in many ways it was my last glimpse of my friend, Marie. Not only the last Queen of France but Maria Antonia, a rose in whose environment none other could thrive.

Desdemona Draws a Breath

Nelly:

Aright sir? I saw you looking. Like what you see? Nah, don't turn away, I'm not one of them girls, I'm a proper actress. Been in the Gaiety 'ave you? Then you'll have seen me – quite a lot of me – on the stage. Yeah, that was me, it was only the smoke from the lime lights making me cough, honest. Don't go sir, I'm sure you'd like a little company and I need what's in your pocket. I was always meant to be an actress. It was my destiny, ever since I saw Desdemona die.

At a fair, after the assizes, it was, a girl in a white nightie was strangled by a dark man inside a tent while they hanged the pick-pockets and horse thieves outside. It turned out later that she was just a barmaid and her husband had caught her with another bloke but she'll always be Desdemona to me.
I went out into the summer night as they were cutting down the dead and saw my fortune spread out before me. Beneath the stars I saw other lights, I walked among the hanging crowd knowing they would be my audience and all would know my name.

Wait a little sir, it's only the night air. I can do a good Cleopatra if you've got the snake for it, wouldn't you like to hear me die sir? It's not my fault, sir. When I went home that night and told how I wanted to be an actress my father chucked me out while me old mum wept for shame. So I went method; what's a girl to do, sir? Variety's yet to come but if it hasn't made me versatile, it's made me flexible and I can give you on my knees what Salome offered only on a platter. How about it then, sir? Will you come to bed, my lord?

The Anchoress

Agnetha:

The Office of the Dead continues, its ringing tone slips between the cold stones of the church and settles with those buried below. I force myself to remain inert, as is becoming to a corpse, even a breathing one, as it passes from the life it has known. I think of that life; hands grasping in the dark; too many hungry eyes on me, and my fortune. A rich girl is no freer than a poor one; not when she has lands in her dowry. Look at my uncle, the bishop, standing there. Is he sorry for my choice to leave the world? Or simply that my lands; those rich and fertile lands next to his own, were not part of my payment to this parish? He should have considered what arrows I still had in my quiver when he forced me to my knees in front of him when I asked my favour. His oft-professed love for me took on a very different hue in that interview.

The taste of him still lingers in my mouth. Yet the favour was granted and I have taken my vow; I will remain here in this cell. I am an Anchoress, a living saint, and I will be left to decay in piety without the corruption the world demands.
Above this endless chanting, I hear birdsong and my heart breaks. The natural world thrums around me in all its sustaining beauty. Oh God, that I must be dead to this world that is so full of life and colour! Yet what alternative can there be?

My parents are dead and there are too many wolves in the forest.

My uncle's voice takes on a mournful tone as I am led into my tomb. A bed, an altar and a crucifix. I deliberately do not face the door as it is sealed though I flinch as the bishop added his mark.
The rite is over. I am committed but I am safe. There is a hatch in the church-side window for my food. Today my uncle himself pushes through my fare of bread and wine.
"Forgive me. I was weak for you are fair."
I take the goblet and swirl the wine around in my mouth, its sweetness replaces the bitter taste this world has left. My eyes pierce him until he lowers his own and then I turn to my night-soil bucket, and spit.

Men

After Arras, Heading West

Temporary Chaplain to the Forces, Reverend Thomas Farley, began the war with such high hopes. Following the Battle of Arras he is a broken man.

Reverend Thomas Farley:

Every man believes in something. As a boy the world was a simple place. I believed in God and the Empire was heaven on earth. It was an exciting time to be alive. There was the motor car, then a lunatic turned genius and we had powered flight. There was so much to delight in, so much to congratulate ourselves for. And above it all, there was the simple, honest belief that Britain ruled the world, God was an Englishman and Jerusalem a Sussex lea. How many men went to war for that idea of England? That was what they fought for: we were the centre of the world and we felt ourselves threatened. It was a righteous war against tyranny: decreed by government, justified by faith.

Every man must believe in something. The night I spent in that prison cell was the longest of my life. The prisoner wasn't a Boche but a private from a London battalion who had refused to fight. He wept for his mother when I explained what would happen at dawn. In all my well-practised assurances of life-everlasting I could find no words to comfort him. In the long cold hours before dawn he did not sleep but watched the night pass, taking with it the remaining moments of his life. I watched with him and I saw the emotion wrought on that young face by the morning clamour of the birds outside. But as the darkness gave way to that dreadful light he began to sing, *Onward, Christian soldiers, marching as to* war, softly at first, then louder. He knew it was the last song he would ever sing, *With the cross of Jesus, going on before...* He wanted me to sing with him but the words stuck in my throat. I could not. I could not. He stopped singing and looked at me. In the silence we heard the sound of boots outside then the clatter of keys. We stood facing each other, listening to the Empire's terrible approach. It was time.

I have never known a more beautiful dawn. A fine mist lingered below what was left of the trees and I remembered those morning runs at school when the air was pure and the world our own. The prisoner walked beside me, the damp grass giving our boots a shine any soldier would have been proud of. I do not know if he heard me as I recited the prayer, perhaps he no longer cared, but a man should believe in something. I lingered while they tied the blindfold then I whispered, "Safe in the arms of Jesus", and my duty was done. At the end of the field the soldiers had had lined up, as though they were about to choose teams. At the command they took aim. The boy leapt and died without a sound and I was finished.

They will be here soon. I do not have to wait until

dawn. I shall sail with the convoy, to England. They tell me that I will recover. They tell me that this war is just. If only a man could believe in something.

Bounced

A nightclub bouncer stands outside the door of a slightly seedy club. A drunk is trying to gain entry to the club. Jeff's having none of it. Throughout the scene Jeff is the only one who speaks.

Jeff: Nah mate, I'm not saying you can't come in. All I'm saying is that your trainers can't come with you. I don't care if they're Nikes, they're not coming in, company policy; no trainers. I know mate, it's a bugger, but what can you do?

The drunk sits down on the grounds and takes his trainers off.

Jeff: Ah, now that's not nice. This is a nightclub mate, the only thing that's cheesy about this place is the music and that's the way the owner likes it. You know what I'm saying? Jesus...

Another man enters and bends down to talk to the drunk with the trainers.

Jeff: 'Ere, you 'is mate? Take him for a kebab or summink will ye? See if you can dry him out a bit...and get him to pick up his Nikes

The second man remonstrates with Jeff.

Jeff: I'm not interested, mate. Just do it.

The two drunks raggedly leave the stage. Jeff watches them go and then addresses the audience.

Jeff: This isn't what I was meant for. I was born to tread the boards. (Striking a pose) "Oh that this too sullied flesh would melt..." (another pose) "The barge she sat in, like a burnish'd throne, Burnt on the water. The poop was beaten gold, Purple the sails, and so perfumèd that..." (sniffs, drops pose). All those years spent studying: endless Sunday afternoons of homework when I could have been up the park with a bottle of White Lightning and friends... While I could have been getting high I was getting Donne, and Marvel, and Herrick. While I should have been shagging my way around London I was reading about nineteenth century poets shagging their way around London - Romantic my arse - It's just not right; I mean, look at me, what stands before you is talent. Talent in its purest, highest form. You only have to see me to know that there is more ability just waiting to be squeezed from this little finger than currently exists in the entire *dramatis personae* of the RSC.

But it's always the same old story. I don't look the part. It's always; "Very good, darling. But I simply can't see you as

Caesar; one look at you and Brutus would have thought better of it." I am surrounded and confounded by pretty boys and petty men all conspiring against me for my lack of looks. Bastards. Don't go thinking I don't get parts: oh I get parts, I've been miners and murderers, doormen and lawmen, corpses and couriers and I've played boatmen and barmen until I was pulling oars and pints in my sleep. But I am a man of many parts and I deserve a part that speaks! I've sacked my agent. He didn't appreciate what he had in me, promised me the earth and gave me nothing but dust. I decided I'd be better off on me own. I mean, how hard can it be? (*Pause)* So I'm "resting" which really means I'm working every hour God sends to pay the rent; that's why I'm here, keeping these oiks out of the club while I'm waiting for the phone to ring. Nothing yet; the *rest* is silent, ha ha. Yeah well, I never said I was a comic.

A clubber staggers out of the club and slumps down against the wall.

Jeff: Alright there mate? Yeah you sit down there until you can stand up again. What's that? Seeing stars? We're all seeing stars mate, but they're a long way from this gutter.

He's Gone

The brother of the victim swears revenge.

Danny:

When I was a kid I really looked up to my brother. He was the captain of the school football team and all my mates thought he was really cool. They thought I was cool too because he was my brother and he'd let me hang around with him, even when his mates were there.

Nothing ever seemed to bother him. "A calming influence" mum called him. When our dad walked out I didn't handle it too well. I kept getting into trouble at school. When I was suspended for fighting mum was so ashamed she wouldn't come up to the school to collect me. It was Jon who came to fetch me. He didn't say a word all the way home. I was expecting to get a bollocking. I deserved to get one but when we got home he just looked at me rather sadly and asked if I was alright. I couldn't look at him. I couldn't explain how I was feeling inside. That weekend he took me camping. I'll always remember that warm, summer's night we spent laying out under the stars, just him and me. He didn't ask about what had happened at school, or how I felt about dad going but he listened when I needed to talk. It made me feel better. That tense, angry feeling started to go away.

He was the first person in our family to go to

university. My mum was so proud of him she couldn't stop telling people. She threw a big party and invited all the neighbours. I think Jon was embarrassed by the attention but he let mum have her moment. I got drunk that night. I didn't want him to go and I drank until I was sick. He sat with me in the bathroom and promised he'd be back at Christmas. Christmas! That was nearly three months away, it seemed such a long time. It sounds silly now.

The Saturday he was due to come home mum went down the shops a bought a Victoria sponge, Jon's favourite. We were going to have a special tea to celebrate him coming home. He didn't come. All evening mum kept going to the window to look out for him. "Come on Jon!" she kept saying but every time she said it her voice sounded tighter, more frightened. By the time the ten o'clock news finished she'd stopped looking out for him. We just sat and stared at the screen. The telly seemed louder than usual but I could still hear the clock ticking in the hall. I listened to that sound for a long, long time. I suppose I fell asleep for suddenly the place was full of police. They seemed too big for our front room in their fluorescent jackets and flat caps. Everything suddenly looked different, it was like I'd woken up in someone else's house. There was broken china everywhere and the cake had gone up the wall. There was jam and cream smeared all down the wallpaper. I looked around for mum "Look what someone's done to Jon's cake," I wanted to say but she wasn't there. Mum wasn't there, just this woman I didn't know, screaming and crying and rocking herself backwards and forwards, all at the same time. A policewoman was sitting with her, trying to say something but this woman kept screaming for her baby. Someone had taken her baby.

It was only when my dad turned up that they told me Jon had been killed. The police said they had him on CCTV getting a bus up from town. It was a journey we'd both made a thousand times but this time there'd been a gang of four or five boys hanging around the bus stop. From the CCTV it looked like he'd brushed against one of them getting off the bus. It could happen to anyone, it didn't mean anything but they went after him. Honour had to be satisfied and one of them had a knife. They left him lying out under the stars on a cold winter's night, all alone. He was ten minutes from home. The police never found who did it but I will. I had the best brother a kid could wish for and they left him to die alone. Now they think they can just go on as though nothing's happened. But something has happened. It's happened to us and I'll find them. I'll find them and I'll make them wish they'd never been born. Who's going to stop me? Jon's not here anymore.

It's Too Late Now

Jon's killer wishes he could turn the clock back.

Ches:

We weren't enemies or nothing; I didn't even know him. I'm not a killer! I'm not like that! I mean, I'm cool an' that, people know they don't mess wi' me but not this. Not this! Yeah, I'm in a gang. Just a few mates, we've known each other since primary school. We look out for each other, man. No big deal, just hanging out, listening to music you know? We weren't trying to intimidate no one but it's not safe to go off the estate so we stayed close.

I don't know who got a knife first. There was this guy I didn't know too well. Somebody's cousin I think. I didn't like him. I mean, it was my gang but he was always dissing me, trying to make out I was a kid, you know? Well one day he brought out this knife. He backed me up against the wall and held it to my throat, in front of everyone. I was shitting myself, man, but he just laughed. Just messin' he said but after that we all had knives. We wanted to feel safe. This new bloke was always on my back, making comments, saying I was weak an' that. There were even talk about some of them going off with him in a new gang.
We were hanging around the bus stop. It was nearly Christmas and we were bored. I wanted to go home, it was cold and dark and I didn't feel all that but I knew I couldn't. I knew he was watching

me, waiting for his chance to take over. Anyway, the bus come along and a couple of people got off. One of them had a big rucksack. It must have been heavy because as he jumped down he stumbled into me. He said "Sorry, mate" and walked on. He stumbled! I know it was an accident, I think I knew it then as well but I couldn't let it go. The boys were watching me, if I'd done nothing I'd have lost everything. I went after him, I shouted something – I don't know what. He turned; I can still see the surprise on his face. I hit him. I hit him hard, twice. We were standing under a streetlight and I suddenly saw his face go white. I looked down and there was a knife in my hand. I 'ain't never seen so much blood. I just stood and stared at him as he choked on the blood coming out of his mouth. Then he just fell. He was still wearing his backpack so he sort of slumped down on the pavement. It was like he was sitting staring up at me, though his eyes looked weird as though they weren't really seeing anything. There was a strange, whistling sound coming from his throat. My mates had gone. I turned and ran.

Six months. It doesn't feel like six months. It feels like it happened last night. Nothing seems to matter anymore; nothing seems real. I can't stop thinking about it. I wish I could go back and see him get up again. If only there was something I could say or do to make it so it hadn't happened. But I can't. I don't want to talk no more. What's the use? Nothing I say will make any difference. It's too late.

The Confession of Jesus Barrabas

A timely intervention turned one young killer's life around.

Barrabas:

Who's that in the shadows? Show yourself! Oh, it's you, Joachim. I've been waiting for you. You were so angry when you left... I was afraid. Why do you stand in the dark? Step into the light so that I can see you. There's a knife in your hand. I see blood; oh Joachim, was it really worth that?

Don't turn away from me, boy. No! You are wrong to dismiss me. You think I am a feeble-minded old man, that I know nothing of what you feel but let me tell you this: when I was your age I too was without friends. I was the son of a Samaritan whore, doubly an outcast. No one cared for me and I cared for no one else. One quiet afternoon I became a murderer. I slit a man's throat for money. That's all there was to it. He had money, I didn't. I wanted it and I took it. He bled a lot for a thin man; that incriminating crimson soaked into my homespun and proclaimed me a killer. I should have fled the city. It would have been easy enough if I'd gone quickly but I needed comfort and my flesh was weak. I spent the money I had stolen on a prostitute named Rebekah. There was nothing she wouldn't do for five denarii (beat) and no one she wouldn't betray for ten.
So I was snatched from a warm, and very satisfied, sleep by what seemed like the entire Roman army

and dragged in front of the Procurator. In those days it was a man called Pontius Pilate. He deserved his end, I can tell you. The bastard sentenced me to crucifixion without even looking at me. To him I was something less than human. You've seen crucifixions, Joachim, barbaric punishments for barbarians. No Roman is ever crucified.

I cannot describe how it feels to be under the sentence of death. I had found it easy enough to take a life but I clung to mine. I had been arrested just before Passover and from my cell I could hear the crowd celebrating. I hated that crowd; they knew nothing of me and they cared less. I was utterly alone. When at last they swung open the door of my cell everything went; my wits, my legs. My bowels. I was dragged, stinking of shit and terror, to where Pilate addressed the crowd. There was another man, also chained. I could see at once that he had been beaten. His whole body trembled with the effort of keeping to his feet. A circlet of thorns had been forced onto his head and beneath his blood-stiffened hair, the skin was bruised and swollen. This was the man who had called himself a king, who had challenged Roman rule. You know what the Romans are like, Joachim. They like to humiliate. Even that poor sod, under sentence of crucifixion, had to be put in his place before they nailed him to it. I didn't think he'd noticed me; he was withdrawn, as though in silent communion with himself. I wondered at his strength. Then Pilate raised his voice and asked the crowd which of us he should release. Release! I felt myself stagger beneath this cruel hope. For I could not ignore it, this new and unlooked for chance of life! But cruel it was for how could I, a proved murderer, hope to be chosen over a man who had done nothing but speak out of turn? Our given names were the same. I listened to the crowd chanting "Jesus, Jesus!" with mounting despair. This hope was none at all. Then all of a sudden I heard my own name. The sound filled my ears and the air seemed to ring with it. For they were not crying "Jesus of Nazareth" as I had thought but Jesus Barrabas, Barrabas, Barrabas! Pilate, too, seemed perplexed for he pointed at the young man and shouted "What am I to do with him?" "Crucify him!" came the answer. "Crucify him!"

Soldiers seized us both and dragged us out of the mid-day sun into a cold, stone corridor. To the right lay liberty. To the left: release of a different kind. The young man never said a word. Oh Joachim, it wasn't my cowardice that made me a better man but something that happened in that shadowy passage. For as we passed each other in the half-light the young man turned his head and looked at me, outcast though I was. It could only have been for a minute but the world seemed to stand still. He smiled, Joachim. He was on his way to death and he smiled at me, a murderer.

Unisex

An Epic Settlement

A parody of the Jason / Medea story. The divorce is hostile to say the least.

Litigius / Litigia:

Ah, Mr Kostalopodus, do sit down. Who? My secretary? I'm sorry if she upset you. She is rather bad-tempered, a bit of a gorgon I'd say. Not to her face, of course, ha ha! Of course I'm joking, Mr Kostalopodus. But don't catch her eye. Just in case. Now then, to business: I am afraid my client is not entirely happy with the divorce proceedings. No, she is not challenging the grounds. I have convinced her, at great length I might add, that your client has grounds to cite unreasonable behaviour. She is, however, dissatisfied with the settlement your client is offering. Of course the custody of the children is now, regrettably, a moot point. However, there are certain items, of personal sentimental value, that my client feels should be included in the final settlement. (Listens) Well, of course; my client has instructed me to negotiate on her behalf but there is one point on which she will not compromise. This is a certain sheepskin wall hanging of a golden hue... what? Yes I think it might be called a fleece if you want to use the agricultural term. Either way, it is very dear to my client. (Listens, interrupts) I appreciate its value, Mr Kostalopodus, but my client is gaining very little in this divorce, particularly when you consider what she gave up for the marriage. She is finding it very traumatic indeed. Up until now your client has led a charmed life but I hardly need remind you that my client was instrumental in acquiring the...er...fleece. After all, she defied her father out of love, yes *love*, Mr Kostalopodus to help your client obtain it. Indeed, I understand that it was this event that led to the loss of my client's beloved brother. Now that was never proved, Mr Kostalopodus. I suggest you don't repeat such allegations unless you...oh, your client may well consider her a poisonous witch with a drug problem but at least she keeps her word. And considering your client swore before all the gods in Olympia to keep faith with my client, I'd say you're skating on very thin ice by representing him. Very thin ice indeed. I'd keep an eye out for lightning bolts if I were you. In fact, wasn't that a rumble of thunder just then? What's that, Mr Kostalopodus? Of course, I've kept you quite long enough. Good to see you again. I'll tell my client she can have the fleece then? Yes, I thought you'd say that. Could you ask my next client to come in? He should be easy to spot. He's the one chained to a boulder. Watch out for the bird.

Sketches & Plays

Fair Nymph

An almost bare stage, sparsely & coldly lit, suggestive of a wasteland. Ophelia, dressed in plain cotton clothes, muddied and torn, staggers on from SR.

Ophelia:

Bloody, bloody men! So busy quarrelling over who misses me the most that they both missed the fact that I am still alive! I came to myself pressed against my brother's chest only to be tumbled back into the cold, dark earth so my darling brother could fight with Hamlet. Hamlet! So clearly mad with grief at my apparent demise that he didn't even look at me. Just wait until I catch up with them. I'm going to kill the pair of them.

Horatio enters with a distracted air. He stops short when he sees Ophelia. Standing with her back to him, she remains unaware of his presence until he speaks.

Horatio: Here's unlooked for company, but what maid is this?

Ophelia: Ay me...

Horatio: She speaks!

Ophelia: Look at the state of my nails!

Horatio: How now Madam?

Ophelia: Hmm? Oh, hello Horatio.

Horatio: Angels and ministers of grace defend us!

Ophelia: Horatio

Horatio: Avaunt and quit my sight! Oh will none in Denmark rest quiet in their graves?

Ophelia: Well, I enjoyed the sleep but it's difficult to breathe under six foot of earth.

Horatio: Oh!... Come again?

Ophelia: I am not dead. I was, how shall I put this? Untimely buried.

Horatio: Oh horrible!

Ophelia: Yes it was rather. I had to claw my way out. It has done nothing for my skin, my manicurist will have a fit and look at what I'm wearing!

Horatio: Grave clothes madam!

Ophelia: I can't believe that I've been seen dead in these! Just as well I am still alive, Death wouldn't want a paramour who looks like an awkward sister he can't marry off!

Horatio: The Queen was most anxious that you went to your grave dressed according to your rank.

Ophelia: Remind me to thank her.

Horatio: As to that, my lady, I have words...

Ophelia: Everyone has been behaving very oddly lately. Why did you all think I was dead?

Horatio: The Queen said that, while you were picking flowers by the river, you slipped in and drowned.

Ophelia: That was careless. How did the Queen know? Was she there?

Horatio: I don't know, my lady.

Ophelia: I quite like the idea of her wading in to fish me out. She needs cooling down. Like a bitch on heat that one.

Horatio: (*Aside*) She's cold now. (*To Ophelia*) How are you?

Ophelia: Well, I'm not dead.

Horatio: No, I meant the...ah...other thing.

Ophelia: What other thing?

Horatio: Before you...er... seemed to drown, you were not...er...not yourself.

Ophelia: Mad, you mean?

Horatio: Um...yes.

Ophelia: That is typical of the judgemental attitude at Court. I sing one dirty song in front of the Queen and suddenly I find myself under the doctor.

Horatio: They thought only to help you, my lady.

Ophelia: In a way they did. He was very good.

Horatio: So what now my lady? Shall I attend you back to Court?

Ophelia: Thank you, Horatio, but no. My thoughts fly to Norway.

Horatio: Norway!

Ophelia: I have given up on Hamlet. I thought he loved me once but it has become clear to me that he is still in thrall to his mother. He just doesn't fancy me.

Horatio: He must be mad.

Ophelia: He tried to pretend he was. All that looming around the castle in a state of undress, sighing deeply and messing about with actors: what a performance! It was quite insulting really, all he needed to say was, "look darling, it was good but it's over now". He was a very selfish man.

Horatio: Hush, my lady. You must not speak ill of the...

Ophelia: ...Sweet Prince? Such loyalty does you justice, Horatio. He was good once: a scholar and a courtier both. But, since my burial, I find that my taste has matured a little. Now I want a man who wants me; desires me to distraction. A man who knows what to do with his...sword. Now, the young Fortinbras strikes me as just such a man. He will take according to his desire, not his conscience.

Horatio: My lord Hamlet has lately fought a duel.

Ophelia: I never knew he had it in him. He must have been surprised into it. Who did he fight? Was it anyone I know?

Horatio: Your brother, my lady, good Laertes.

Ophelia: Good! Hah! That's a joke. You should have seen some of the postcards he sent me from Paris. So, they fought each other? Was either hurt?

Horatio: Both, my lady.

Ophelia: Badly?

Horatio: Quite badly, yes.

Ophelia: Horatio?

Horatio: They're dead my lady.

Ophelia: No! Wait a minute, are you sure? You've been wrong before.

Horatio: Quite sure my lady, they were poisoned.

Ophelia: Both of them? In a duel?

Horatio: And the King and Queen.

Ophelia: Blimey. What is left at Court?

Horatio: Nothing, nothing...

Ophelia: My poor brother....

Horatio: (*Continues to speak, apparently oblivious that she is speaking*) ...nothing....

Ophelia: I always thought him a bit of a...

Horatio: ...nothing...

Ophelia: Hot head. But I... (*looks at Horatio expectantly*)

Horatio: Nothing

Ophelia: ...shall miss him. Poor Hamlet. Silly sod. It's a strangely finite end for one so vacillating.

Horatio: I would have followed him to the grave but he said I must stay alive to give a good account of him to Fortinbras.

Ophelia: Fortinbras? Why should he care?

Horatio: He's just invaded Denmark

Ophelia: You mean, he's here?

Horatio: He is at Elsinore now, taking an inventory of the furniture.

Ophelia: Then take me to him. I must throw myself on his... mercy.

Horatio: But, my lady, he is our enemy.

Ophelia: Then I shall die in his arms. Come Horatio; stand not upon your scruples but let us go at once.

(*Exeunt*)

Empty Box Sketch

Performed at the Red Lion Theatre, Islington, London, for "Writers Bloc" on Monday 2nd July 2012.

An old-fashioned shop counter.

Customer:	Hello, I'd like a box of your deluxe fireworks please.
Shopkeeper:	Certainly sir.
Customer:	This feels very light.
Shopkeeper:	That's because it's empty, sir.
Customer:	Empty? Where are the fireworks?
Shopkeeper:	We don't sell them.
Customer:	But you have them there in the window.
Shopkeeper:	We have the boxes sir. There aren't any fireworks in them.
Customer:	Well yes, I appreciate that

you use empty boxes for display...

Shopkeeper: Not just display, sir.

Customer: What?

Shopkeeper: This is an empty box shop.

Customer: You mean you *sell* empty boxes?

Shopkeeper: That's right, sir. Every box you see here is empty.

Customer: Even the cereal boxes?

Shopkeeper: Especially those sir. Here we have Shredded Wheat

Shopkeeper: And Cornflakes?

Customer: And you actually make a living at this?

Shopkeeper: A roaring trade, sir.

Customer: Who buys empty boxes?

Shopkeeper: Oh you'd be surprised, sir. We get a lot of interest from school children.

Customer: Really?

Shopkeeper: Yes sir, Maths projects, science projects. Also the students who want to play on parental sympathies in the hopes of a handout. Then of course there's the Blue Peter crowd.

Customer: Blue Peter?

Shopkeeper: A trifle hippy now, that whole make do and mend thing, but when it comes to empty washing up liquid bottles, we struggle to meet demand, we really do. Sir? Are you alright sir?

Customer: (*pointing at a space rocket on the shelf behind shopkeeper)* I once made a space rocket just like that.

Shopkeeper: Did you sir?

Customer: Years ago now. When I was - happy. May I hold it? Just for a moment?

Shopkeeper: Of course sir.

Customer: Oh.

Shopkeeper: Sir?

Customer: This brings back memories.

Shopkeeper: It takes a lot of people like that sir. Perhaps you would like to make another one? We have a playroom just through that curtain there.

Customer: Well, really, I don't know...

Shopkeeper: Go on sir, just through there. Valerie will look after you. We're very discreet. Oh look, there's one she made earlier. Go on sir, she won't bite.

Customer: Well alright then. Thank you, I will. (*exit*)

Shopkeeper: Same again, Valerie. Just drop the money in the toy box and there'll be crumpet for tea.

Food for Thought

Cast List

Lucy Late 20s / early 30s. English. Perhaps not as demure as she may at first appear.

Graham 30s / early 40s. Successful, expects to get his own way in all things.

Gian-Luca Late 20s / early 30s. Italian. Speaks with a noticeable accent.

Manager 50s / 60s. Italian but perhaps 2nd generation.

NB:

1. The lines of Italian dialogue can also be performed in English. A translation at the end of the script is provided for this purpose.

2. The world "bruschetta" should be pronounced "brusketta". In the play, Lucy consistently pronounces it as "brushetta".

Food for Thought

a play in one act

A young couple are shown to a table in a restaurant. They order wine and the waiter returns with a bottle of wine and one of water.

Lucy: This is nice. (*Looking around*) Very romantic.

Graham: Well, I thought it would be nice to go somewhere special, as its Valentine's Day. The pizza places are alright but I know how you love Italian cooking.

Lucy: It brings back happy memories of my student days.

Graham: And you've never been back to Siena?

Lucy: No, although I did have a wonderful holiday in Rome a few years ago – just before I met you.

Graham: Perhaps we can go back together some time.

Lucy: Hmm, I'd like that.

As they are speaking, the waiter arrives. He is

rather bored but still polite.

Gian-Luca: You would like to order something?

Graham: Go ahead, darling, I like to hear you speak Italian.

Lucy: (*to Gian-Luca)* Hi, I'd like the bruschetta di Pomodoro, per favore. (*She pronounces bruschetta as "brushetta")* Followed by the sgombro grigliato con la salsa verde.

Gian-Luca: (*automatically correcting her as he writes down the order to sound the "k" sound)* Bruschetta di pomodoro. (*He looks up at her and can't take his eyes off her).*

Lucy: All that time in Italy and I can't pronounce the simplest thing.

Graham: I still love you. (*To Gian-Luca*) And I'd like- (*Gian-Luca is staring at Lucy and doesn't hear him).* And I'd like.

Gian-Luca: Scusa, yes sir?

Graham: I'd like the *verdure griglate con caprino* followed by the Milanese (*he also makes a poor job of the pronunciation, Gian-Luca tries not to wince).*

Gian-Luca: Thank you, sir. (*He collects the menus and exits, still staring at Lucy*)

Graham: Strange chap. Now then, where were we?

Lucy: A special occasion?

Graham: Ah, possibly. My lips are sealed.

Lucy: You won't give me just a little hint?

Graham: Oh Lucy, I know very well that you wouldn't be satisfied with a little one.

Graham's phone rings

Lucy: You didn't switch it off? Not even on Valentine's Day?

Graham: Sorry, darling. The thing is I'm waiting for a rather important call.

Lucy: Oh, I see.

Graham: You know I wouldn't normally but, in this case, it's make or break...

Lucy: Ok ok, just answer it before they ring off!

Graham: Sorry. (*Answering phone*) Hello?

	Giles! Yes... (*Gets up and exit. Gian-Luca enters*)
Gian-Luca:	Verdure...?
Lucy:	(*Pointing to Graham's place*) Oh that's there.
Gian-Luca:	And the...
Lucy:	Bruschetta, yes, that's me.
Gian-Luca:	Say it again.
Lucy:	What? Bruschetta. (*At this point Gian-Luca leans forward and kisses her passionately)* Get off! What the...
Gian-Luca:	(*Sitting in Graham's seat*) I knew it was you, Lucia! Oh how I have dreamed of, longed for this moment.
Lucy:	I'm sorry, I think you've mistaken me for someone else.
Gian-Luca:	No, no mistake. How could I forget you, carissima? From the moment I saw you in the Campo dei Fiori on that summer evening all those years ago...
Lucy:	How many years ago?

Gian-Luca: What does time matter in affairs of the heart? Every moment without you has been an eternity. (*Seizes her hand, leans closer to gaze soulfully into her eyes. She tugs her hands away as Graham returns*)

Graham: Er, excuse me?

Gian-Luca: What? Oh yes. (*Reluctantly gets up and resumes gazing at Lucy*).

Graham sits down and looks at his dinner.

Graham: Got any black pepper?

Gian-Luca: Hmm? Oh, I suppose so... *He exits briefly then returns with the pepper mill and grates it over Graham's plate, still staring at Lucy*)

Graham: Thank you. Thank you. That's enough now. Stop it! (*Gian-Luca offers pepper to Lucy. She shakes her head and he leaves*). Well, he's not getting a tip.

Lucy: Poor man, he thinks I'm his lost love.

Graham: You're not are you?

Lucy: It's hard to say, there were so many...

Graham: What?

Lucy: I'm kidding. No, it's not me. He's talking about some girl he met in the Campo dei Fiori. It's pretty popular with foreign students.

Graham: Campo dei what?

Lucy: *dei Fiori*, in Rome. It means "Field of the Flowers". There's a lovely pub there called The Drunken Ship. I'll show you when we go.

Graham: I can't wait. How's your food?

Lucy: Wonderful! I wish I could make tomatoes on toast taste this good. How's yours?

Graham: Peppery. Listen, I must confess I had an ulterior motive for bringing you here tonight.

Lucy: Oh?

Graham: Yes, there's...er something I've been wanting to ask you.

He brings out a ring box. Lucy puts her hands to her mouth.

Lucy: Oh my God!

Graham gets up, moves stage front and kneels

down in front of Lucy. Gian-Luca arrives with the main courses. He puts one plate down in Graham's place, making it obvious that he is looking for him. Then he puts the other plate in front of Lucy smiling at her. He realises that she's looking at Graham as he kneels in front of her and puts a ring on her finger.

Gian-Luca: What are you doing?

Lucy: He has just asked me to marry him. And... and I've said yes!

Gian-Luca tears around the table, pushes Graham over and pulls the ring off Lucy's finger and throws it at Graham. He holds Lucy's hands in his own and kneels before her as Graham has just done.

Gian-Luca: No, Lucia, you can't do this to me. We have only just found each other after all this time. You must not throw yourself away on him. There is no need. I am here now.

Lucy: You're mad. This is my boyfriend. I want to marry him. You have ruined a very romantic moment.

Gian-Luca: But we will have lots of romantic moments, together.

Lucy: Look, I am not who you think I am.

Gian-Luca: Yes you are! How could you think I

would forget?

Graham: (*Picking up the ring*) Where's the manager? I want to see the manager.

Gian-Luca: Why you want the manager? This doesn't concern him, you must deal with me!

The two men start to square up to each other.

Lucy: Oh now stop it! This is ridiculous.

The manager enters

Manager: I understand that there's a problem here?

Graham: Your waiter just attacked me. He should be sacked.

Manager: Gian-Luca? But he is a good boy. One of my best workers. (*To Luca)* Che é successo qui? Hai veramente attaccato questo signore?

Gian-Luca: Che altro posso fare? Lui ha rubato il mio amore!

Manager: Il tuo amore? Una raggazza?
Gian-Luca: Certo una ragazza!

Manager: Dov'é lei? (*Pointing at Lucy)*

Questa signora?

Gian-Luca: Sí, questa donna é l'amore della mia vita.

Manager: Signora, do you know this man?

Lucy: No, he is just a waiter who has ruined what should have been a romantic proposal. It should have been a special moment in my life and instead my fiancé has just been knocked to the ground a by an over-amorous waiter. It's hardly every girl's dream.

Manager: I am very sorry, signora. (*To Gian-Luca*) Gian-Luca, you must apologise.

Gian-Luca: Never! He has stolen my woman! I challenge him to a dual! (*He seizes a fork*)

Graham: With a fork?

Gian-Luca: (*Passionately*) Sí! One plate of spaghetti and two forks. Mangiamo. L'uno contro l'altro. I know I will win: the English are incapable of eating spaghetti without a spoon!

Silence. Manager, Lucy and Graham stare at Gian-Luca . He lowers his fork.

Lucy: (*To Graham)* I think we should just go.

They get up and start to put on coats &c. The manager fusses about them.

Manager: I really am most sincerely sorry, please do accept my apologies. Perhaps you will come back another time, on the house of course...

The manager continues to fuss around Graham as Lucy goes over to Gian-Luca.

Lucy: Please believe me, I am not the person you think I am

Gian-Luca: I was so sure. I could never forget her. No one ever danced the Macarena like her.

Lucy: It's a group dance.

Gian-Luca: I know, but there was just something about the way she swung her arms (*he imitates the movements of the Macarena*) I came all the way from Italy to find her.

Lucy: I hope you do find her. (*Turning away*)

Gian-Luca: She is fixed in my heart and *in* my memory. The girl in the Union Jack dress. She was such a fan of the Spicey Girls. I still have that dress. Treasured memories. Ah well. Forgive me, signora and congratulations.

(*exit*)

Lucy: I wondered where I'd left that! Oh my God!

Graham: (*entering)* Are you ready?

Lucy: What? Oh, yes.

Graham: Let's go home. We can ring for a pizza.

Gian-Luca comes back and starts to clear the table. He is laying out fresh covers when Lucy returns.

Gian-Luca: Did you forget something, signora?

Lucy: Yes. My dress.

Gian-Luca looks at her and, wordlessly *Lucy reaches up and kisses him. He is stunned. She then tucks a piece of paper into his breast pocket.*

Lucy: Call me.

(*exit*)

Blackout

Translation of the Italian on page 7

Manager: Gian-Luca? But he is a good boy. One of my best workers. (*To Luca)* Che é successo qui? Hai veramente attaccato questo signore?

Gian-Luca? But he is a good boy. One of my best workers. (*To Luca)* What has happened here? Did you really attack this gentleman?

Gian-Luca: Che altro posso fare? Lui ha rubato il mio amore!

What else could I do? He has stolen my love!

Manager: Il tuo amore? Una raggazza?

Your love? A girl?

Gian-Luca: Certo una ragazza!

Of course a girl!

Manager: Dov'é lei? (*Pointing at Lucy)* Questa signora?

Where is she? (*Pointing at Lucy)* This woman?

Gian-Luca: (*Emotionally)* Sí, questa donna é l'amore della mia vita.

(*Emotionally*) Yes, this woman is the love of my life.

Gian-Luca: (*Passionately*) Sí! One plate of spaghetti and two forks. Mangiamo. L'uno contro l'altro. I know I will win: the English are incapable of eating spaghetti without a spoon!

(*Passionately)*Yes! One plate of spaghetti and two forks. We eat. One against the other. I know I will win: the English are incapable of eating spaghetti without a spoon!

Note to performers:

This is a book of performance pieces intended for use. For audition purposes you may adapt the text to suit your own purposes. However, for public performances the texts must be performed as written unless prior permission has been obtained.

Performance is permitted on the understanding that the author is properly notified and credited.

Bespoke monologues are available from the author for a fee. For further details, or if you have any other comments or suggestions, please e-mail:

quickbeampress@gmail.com

www.ingramcontent.com/pod-product-compliance
Ingram Content Group UK Ltd.
Pitfield, Milton Keynes, MK11 3LW, UK
UKHW041845200726
13854UKWH00005BA/2072

9 780992 770983